the moon, my mind.

ava lawrey

i hope you know it will be okay. it always is.

we grow in darkness.

Copyright

Title book: the moon, my mind

Author: Ava Lawrey

Copyright © 2024, Ava Lawrey

Self-publishing

alawrey36@gmail.com

table of contents

part one:

part two:

poems 181-212

new moon.

01

here you are

it's you versus

the world,

pillow-thinking

your way in

way too deep.

-those pillow thoughts will get you. they will have
you overthinking your entire day over and over
again, creating all these nerves that don't contain
much logic behind them. my challenge to you is to
slow them down.

02

sometimes

things go well

sometimes

they don't—

while i hope your

day was perfect,

i know it wasn't

and that is perfectly

okay.

-perfectionism isn't the goal, contentment is.

03

she spends her day

prancing around with

her heart on her sleeve

allowing emotions to

infiltrate her, wearing

them like a new blouse.

-vulnerability is not weakness

04

the girl who doesn't stay put

the voice of my intuition

is louder than the voice of

just anyone—

i leave without attachment

and follow my inner voice

in hopes to feel belonging

and detachment all at once.

at the end of the day,

people are all living

within themselves—

there's no way they'll

ever know you well

enough to know where

you belong as well as

you know where your

heart belongs

-let these be affirmations for your tomorrow, that you follow where your heart leads you and not allowing anyone to taint your purest desires.

05

night light

fill me in,

she says,

give me

what i

needed to

hear today

and didn't.

06

honey, night

light says,

what you

needed to

hear today

but didn't,

is right

inside your

heart if

you listen.

07

stagnation was always my biggest fear

ever since i first learned the meaning

of this word—it holds so much fear

and lack of movement. i hope so

badly that contentment does not turn

into stagnation for you. while it is a

good goal to be content in your life,

you should never give up on the dreams

you have for yourself, they are never

too big to achieve in this lifetime.

08

for me, night time is the best time to reflect. sort through all the emotions you may have held heavy today. make a night time journal for this maybe, or whatever you please. but it is important that you slow down enough to process emotions and not just breeze through them. feel everything through. do not plow through the way you feel because it is uncomfortable to feel—who taught you that anyways?

09

she doesn't need validation anymore.

she validates herself

by seeing the beauty within

her own skin

again

and again

so, you can fuck off now

she finally learned

what's right

and what's toxic

-self-taught

10

i've been okay with
temporary people
for most of my life—
i always knew that
most people who
come into your life
have an expiration
date and will leave
at some point but
i think what is most
special about life is
finding those some
people that will
come and never have
to leave, it will all
make so much more
sense when they
fit right in

without forcing

it to make sense

because it fits

into your dream

plot.

this isn't a book

though, it's your

life.

11

don't spend any more time
regretting anything that
once made you so happy,
it was good for the plot,
just not good for you now.

12

i'm not sure where i'm going

or even the direction i'm

headed in

i just know that everyday

i keep moving and when i

look back, i've grown from

where i left off

i think that's what matters—

is that you continue to move

even when you have no direction,

no guidance, on what the right

move is.

sometimes you don't know

where you're trying to reach

until you get there.

13

you spend too much time on everyone
else

and not near enough time on yourself

why?

14

it is not selfish to love yourself

and spend time in your own

relationship with yourself

-i hate that social media has made us feel like it is
so bad to take care of ourselves, that it makes us
selfish to put ourselves first. in what world is it not
okay to check up on yourself and cherish the
person you are?

15

late night questions

could you not have stuck around for me?

was i not good enough for you?

when will my time be?

how can i stop being stupid?

when will i learn my lesson?

why is life not fair?

why am i so alone?

16

what your late-night answers should be

i am okay with the fact you left, there's a reason for it.

i was always enough; i am complete as is.

my time will come, just like everyone else's will; the universe is waiting for my moment.

i am not stupid. i have gone through a lot and i am a strong and intelligent individual. a lot of things that happen are simply out of my control.

i will learn my lesson when i allow my heart to open up more, when i heal from the things i have suppressed. until then, these scenarios will repeat so i can learn this lesson.

life isn't fair and that isn't for you to figure out. everything always ends up working out, and you know that.

embrace solitude with open arms, and grow from it. learn yourself so you can let others in again. it is a good thing, and i know you will see that soon.

17

what's the use?

continuing to fight your own mind

ignoring all the signs of growth

all signs of your intuition

coming to surface

what's the use

of running from who you are

and chasing the world?

-let it all go, all of the expectations.

18

the moon is glistening outside,

through the curtain—

she's checking on your heart

and singing you a lullaby—

listen in on the soft noises

of the nighttime

and get the rest you deserve

-goodnight

19

to put you at ease, there's nothing about today you
could have changed. it is too late now, but not in a
bad way. it is supposed to comfort you that they
day is done, that you have lived through another
day. i'm not sure if today was hard on your spirit,
but i do know that you lived through it. good job.

20

at the end of it all,

you're here—

still breathing,

your body still works,

let your mind stop running

so fast,

just listen to your breath

-sometimes i have to calm myself down, focusing
outwards and not inwards. leaving my brain to let
my brain breathe too.

21

you will not ever fail

at whatever it is

if you never stop trying—

someday it will make sense,

maybe it wasn't today

but i hope you trust the universe

enough

22

the same window

that heard the beginnings

heard the ends

heard the cries—

happy and sad.

the light post,

it brought light to darkness

and added light to the fire

-the only light still burning

23

i do not want to be the heartbreaker. the girl who left. i don't want to be a bitch. someone who doesn't care, reckless. i want to be the girl who chose myself through it all. i want to be the one who knew what had to be done and executed it. i don't think it is fair how stories get skewed, and lovers separate.

-the girl who chose herself, who chose happiness. not the reckless one.

24

fuck you fuck you fuck you

how do i move on?

how do we move forward?

but separately

25

i want to scream at the moon.

tell her how much i hate all of it.

tell her how much i hate myself for falling asleep

and having dreams about you

-but i can't. i can't.

26

it comes

it goes

it wanes

and waxes

it's love

and healing

-not linear

27

it'd kill me to move on

it'd kill me to stay

-i should go

28

find peace

there can be unanswered questions

but there can't be anger

let the fuck go

filter inwards

29

as i lay awake at night,

i sink into the thought

that tomorrow is coming too quick

and tomorrow's tomorrow is too soon

i need extra hours in the day

i need extra tomorrows,

more of them

-time is encapsulating and terrifying

30

let me heal from you.

let me take the time each night

to breathe, and on the exhale,

let go of all the suppressed feelings

and things i never confronted

from the old me, the broken me

i think i'm better now

but i haven't stood facing myself

and all the darkness under the moon

and my mind.

waning.

31

if only graduating college

felt like freedom and

less like restraints.

more like money

and less like scarcity.

more opportunities

and less rejections

if only what we worked for

paid off quicker

and left us wondering less.

32

i think it will be okay. i really hope it will.

33

i could sit here and go back to the beginning

debrief every word i ever said,

everything i ever did

but at the end of the day,

 i swore that i would be strong enough

to not look this closely into bad luck—

a lot of people just get dealt bad cards

sometimes.

there's a lot of potentially bad things

that can go wrong in life,

and accepting those things as they come

will help you keep your peace.

-don't overthink the way the universe unfolds.

34

a lot of me is angry

a lot of me is numb though, too.

but tomorrow, my mind will go quiet

as i wake from a deep slumber,

and i will again make the decision to let go,

let the things that are out of my reach,

simply be out of my reach,

35

maybe it was fate,

maybe there were signs i should have followed,

maybe there were people i could have listened to,

or i should have known better,

i could have prevented it.

-or maybe you couldn't have done differently.

find peace in that. i dare you. find peace in allowing life to be shitty sometimes. find peace in knowing that there is tomorrow for those who are blessed to see the day. find peace in knowing through every bad thing that has happened to you so far in life, you have gotten through. and you will continue to get through the bad things that you may think are impossible to get through while you're in the midst of it. but take one thing at a time, moving slowly is better than not moving at all.

37

i think it's good, you know?

going through things, that is.

it teaches you quite a lot about yourself,

your strength,

that's a good thing, right?

growth is one of the best parts about life,

learning new things,

adapting to situations,

and clearing challenges.

38

it's easy to feel alone,

isolate yourself.

it's especially easy when the world does not stop
for you

the universe continues to spin,

classes go on,

and there's only so many personal days you can
take off work.

why doesn't time stop for you?

to everyone else, it's just another day and nothing
significant happened like maybe it did for you.

...

the truth is a lot of people struggle silently,

and quite a lot of people in the world

may be going through something similar,

but you would never get to know that

if you stay silent

39

it's cool though,

that you're here, that is.

i am so proud of you

for every single hardship that you made it through,

good job.

-in case nobody has ever told you.

40

i'm not one to believe in toxic positivity,

ignoring the simple fact that some things suck.

so feel free to sit with me, in rage,

in fear,

in sadness,

in helplessness,

in all of those feelings.

it is okay to feel, here.

41

and i hope that you have a support system,

i hope people don't blind you with positivity,

unsolicited.

i hope there are people out there who allow you

to simply feel,

and drop the front every now and then.

-it is important not to silence others. through
weakness and strength, listening is too easy to not
do for others. having an ear can save lives.

42

i've seen a lot of loss,

physical loss of people

and a mental state of loss, too.

somehow through loss i think

you'll gain something along the way

maybe you'll gain a closer friendship

elsewhere

or maybe,

you will feel a peace of mind

-i hope you wait to see what you gain even through
loss

43

there are a lot of moments that feel empty,

life sucking life out of you like a starving body

the physical pain of emptiness,

while also looming numbness—

sometimes you must fill the void yourself.

44

i hope you hear me when i reassure you. i hope you understand that while nights may be feeling empty as of late, there are so many sunny days coming that you need to live through. you have probably heard me say before that all things are temporary, and they are. that is part of life, whether good or bad. your mind is consistently trying to level your emotions out to neutral, so everything will balance out soon.

-hang in there

45

the gentle hum of the night

rocking you to sleep

tune in and

say goodnight.

46

i think i have mastered it—

the high functioning aspect of it at least.

the unsuspected

the silent

the voiceless

-the ones who fit in and wished they didn't

47

the thing about powering through everything

is that it is unsuspecting

people will pass by and never ask,

you mask being well

so well

just don't fool yourself

48

there is quite a lot of silence

in healing—

like the silence of the night,

the sun wishes to shine bright

49

home is where your heart is

leave your heart to gently beat

in her little home

pressed in-between layers of

love and life

home is where you nurture

not always where was seeded

-feed into the home you want to grow

50

early 20's

spread your love,

it's okay to go far from home

and feel like a child all over again,

rediscovering what makes a home a home

and what makes a heartbeat fast

chase the feeling of youth

allow yourself to slow down,

soak up the freedom

which comes with a great deal of

unknown.

51

being a dreamer

feels cloudy at times,

lost in layers of fog,

uncertainty.

when you dream among the skies,

expect some clouds—

but every plane flies through

clear skies too.

52

learning causes discomfort

if learning was easy,

everyone would be einstein's

-be patient with yourself when you are growing. it takes a lot to learn new patterns and habits, but it also takes a toll when you are just one person, trying to unlearn toxic things you have picked up along the way. but, always keep learning and growing.

53

i hope you take time every day to treat yourself
with kindness. it can be so easy to remember
everyone else and forget about yourself, but i hope
you don't do that. before you took yourself to bed,
i hope you spoke nicely of yourself before you
spend the night in a dream state. i was told your
dreams are much better when you're nice to
yourself.

54

you'll live forever, she said

but only in my poems

where i'll release you

by encapsulating you

in a poem, in a version

of you that will live with me

forever.

55

there was no room for his physicality,

just a thought, a poem,

of him left behind

in words that will never be erased

a legacy, you could say

-left for someone else to stumble into

56

a poet

is just a person

lost in thought,

always

a poet

is just a person

lost in wander

and beauty, too

-life doesn't look the same to a poet, every little
thing has meaning converted into syllables on a
page

57

and when he said sleep tight

darling,

i didn't think he meant to

lock the doors in my heart

and buckle down in my own fear

gasping for air

when he said be safe,

i didn't know he was who i should

be safe from

-i thought it was what he was supposed to say

58

for the longest time
i thought i was invincible
that the world was cruel
but i was not vulnerable
enough to endure that,
i could avoid it—
my heart is made of steel
and protected, somehow.
-naïve.

my heart of steel
crumbled quicker than
expected. remains of
metals and mosaics
of all the experiences
i ever went through,
all within a canvas i
thought was invincible.

it all crumbled so quickly—

there's a puddle on the floor

where my ego shed

and my vulnerability shown through

59

hard times don't discriminate who they let down. unfortunately, everyone has gone through some hard times. the earth doesn't choose who gets let off easily, even though i wish i had some control over the things that happen to me.

60

i hear it knocking on my chest

k

  n

    o

      c

        k

          i

            n

              g

louder and louder

i can't breathe

my heart is racing

i'm going numb

i just wish it would

stop and let me

breathe.

first quarter.

61

be calm,

he said.

it's just me,

he said.

but what he didn't say—

"it's just me",

a person who would

tear my heart out,

one string at a time

almost unnoticeably slow

but overtime, undeniable,

and at the end of it all

allow me to be left out in the

open, exposed, in danger,

in harm's way.

but it's just him, he said.

62

doors shatter behind me

like breaking glass dominoes

sheltering me in quickly,

isolating me from everyone

i once held close

-there's nobody left for me here

63

gone are the days

of cracked windows,

falling asleep to crisp air flowing through

and waking up to birds chirping,

owls hooting—

gone are the days

of false security,

leaving windows unlocked

and doors not triple-checked—

gone are the days

i feared the boogey man

and fabricated tv characters,

getting a tuck-in every night

and sleeping peacefully.

everything changed at some point,

although it's hard to pinpoint when

nights got scary and windows unlocked

were a welcome in for the men who

hunt at night, or maybe even the daytime.

everything changed at some point,

maybe it was the 15 years i grew

or maybe the universe got much more

cruel than i remember back in my

innocence. maybe i still am innocent,

my inner child begging for some air

time, but maybe she is just tainted

by the fears of being a woman in 2023.

-do birds even chirp in the mornings anymore?

64

the breeze at night used

to touch my face softly,

like a gentle kiss from the moon

she used to blanket me in

kindly, gently, peacefully

65

it used to be kind,

my heart, that is,

used to be patient

slow to judge

-what happened to me?

66

don't question it, he said.

but what i really think,

was that i should have questioned it

a whole lot more than i did.

67

was it easy?

faking it until

there was no choice

but to show the shitty

person you truly are.

-must not have been easy.

68

the air turned cold in my heart that night,

even my organs were crying

-i won't forget it

69

i used to be a lot of things,

prior to that of course.

i can't help but mourn

the 20-year-old i was,

full of life, hopelessly romantic,

happily fearless, and overly

eager to begin her 20's.

-wow i am 22 now.

70

but really, is it a bad thing—

that i used to be someone else before all this?
there's got to be something good out of it all, i am
starting to see the good blossom out, but i can't
help to think how bad i wish none of this ever
happened and i could take back time. i want to take
back everything, even the good stuff, from now
until i was 20. i wish i never graduated college yet,
that i didn't feel all that pain. i would trade so many
of my tomorrows to go back in time and change
that part of the plot. two years' worth of confusion
and at this part, i nearly have no recollection of it
even, it just lives in my brain with a sole purpose to
hurt me now and then.

71

i would trade so many tomorrows

to take that back,

rewind and erase as i go.

-i would rather feel nothing.

72

if i could live in your head for a day,

i think it would scare me,

it has to be so dark and frigid,

to have a heart as bad as yours.

73

one thing i love about myself

is my heart,

and i am sure he probably couldn't relate,

but i will always be filled with so much love,

even though he tried to take that from me,

good people don't turn cold.

74

thank god i have something

for myself, something

that i can always promise to

myself.

-i trust myself more than anyone.

75

you have so much to love about yourself—

but when i asked you what your

favorite thing about yourself was,

you looked at me blankly

like nobody had ever asked you,

like you had never even considered

that there are things to love about you

76

-i hope the next person who asks you,

you are eager to explain how much you love

everything about yourself,

all the details you humbly hide,

all the little quirks you have gotten to know,

and from the bottom of my heart,

i hope someone asks you this again.

77

some nights i thrash around

trying to throw away every single thing

that ever touched your forsaken skin,

and damn, it feels like everything i own,

you once touched.

78

please, just go away,

i want a new life now,

a life so far from you

and that pain i felt

79

hello

hello

hell

he

can you hear me?

seems like your mind

is always elsewhere now,

must have been a special

person to have that much

space in your head,

still.

80

i guess maybe we shouldn't be rushing our healing. it doesn't happen overnight, or even over one week. it takes so much patience to learn and heal from what you went through, and that does not make you a weak person. feel everything and feel it deeply. allow it all to arise, even when it is ugly.

81

any day

full of breath,

is a good day.

-i must tell myself this

82

one day

the seconds doubled,

they had to.

there's no way

time feels as if

it's dragging me under,

forcing me to stay

into today

83

there's not much that allows

me to feel things anymore—

somehow, i turned off

the ability to feel.

the music i listen to revives me,

i would be so numb without it

84

the nightmares haven't stopped,

i need to take a breath

but my subconscious

won't allow it.

the gasping hasn't stopped,

it's like the air in my lungs

is constantly being built up,

trapped.

my mind feels like a held breath,

and i just cannot catch up.

-i'm playing catch up with myself.

85

those eyes haunt me,

and not in the hauntingly beautiful way,

in a way that sends shivers down my spine

and takes the breath out of my lungs.

they were sharp—

like daggers sending pain

directly to my heart

they were once kind—

or maybe it was all a part

of my delusions,

or your manipulations.

86

i never thought i was delusional before,

but how could i not after loving someone

so deeply,

who is as bad as you are?

-i should have known.

87

maybe it's the hopeless romantic in me, the way i romanticize everything. even when i shouldn't, i see the good in everyone, in everything. maybe the worst part about me is also the best part about me. the thing people love about me, is the same thing they take advantage of.

88

how could you?

like honestly—

how could

you do

that.

-it is not fair. it never was.

89

it was easier than i thought

to walk away,

i think you opened the door for me

and pushed me out.

90

my phone lit up with a text from you

and my eyes simultaneously lit up

like a chain reaction

it read "happy mother's day"

i squinted confused,

remembering you only texted me that

because you've used me,

seen my body,

sucked on my tits

and expected my heart in return.

i'm drained,

and disrespected

you've taken more than you've given

and i guess that's the core of motherhood,

girlhood even—

immense sacrifice

with no expectation

waxing.

91

reel it in,

give yourself a hug

-it's okay not to be okay, but it's time to take care of yourself.

92

a part of me is still there—

inside those four walls,

stuck in that moment of time—

deep breaths, loud yelling,

a part of me was lost there

the last deep breath i took

was in those four walls.

-i've been holding my breath

93

it was that moment

that changed me

it left such a deep imprint

on my being

and i hope i recover.

94

if i could turn back time,

i'm not even sure i would.

i have to believe that

the sequence of events

that i am given,

is meant for me.

-unfortunately, or fortunately

95

that part of me

isn't here anymore

i am growing

into a new person

96

i still get up every day,

i stay in contact with the people i love,

i work out,

i still read and write,

i eat my meals,

i still laugh and smile,

i do all the things

i slide right past

-my little secret

97

i want to feel important—

not in the way that i should be the smartest,

most beautiful girl in the world,

but i want to be held

without contingencies

i want to be held close to your heart

without sacrificing my own.

i want to be important

in the way you drink your coffee

to get through the day,

even though it isn't an absolute necessity,

your day isn't the same without it

and all you can think about

is the rush it provides

-on your mind and in your heart

98

it wasn't about the materials,

the purchases

the bill at dinner.

it wasn't about the show

or the proving,

any of that.

you had it all wrong

but it was purposeful ignorance.

you wanted me to believe

that you didn't know better,

but now i know

that you did.

-weaponizing ignorance.

99

spin it around,

i beg you.

i plead you to look at it

honestly and thoroughly,

tell me that you deserved that

-i bet you can't

100

it scares me

you know?

moving on.

it just solidifies

that really happened

and i need to make peace

101

there isn't anyone in the world

that would be worth

trading in your pure soul for.

102

one day i looked in the mirror

and saw bits of all the versions

of you i hated the most

staring back at me

i think i took the pieces

of you i didn't want

to make you a better person

-i think it just turned me cold.

103

i wish

the little boy inside you

got nurtured better

so that you would be

a better person today.

104

let me bring you to the beginning,

paint the beautiful image i thought

our love was.

it was overwhelming

the good kind,

full of passion

and adventure.

it was confusing too,

(i ignored that part)

it was the high i was on

that left every bit of

logic behind.

tunnel vision,

and cruising down an open road

it was endless,

full of possibilities

everyone was waiting for it

my soul even was

but it wasn't any of that

without the downfall

before it actually fell,

my heart felt it coming

and i should have listened.

105

the hardest part

is that my heart

still yearns for love

but it's not worth it.

106

i dread the weekdays now,

i spend every day looking

for the courage to make the call

and it reminds me that i'm

still not as strong as i thought.

-my phone knows do not disturb all too well.

107

i lost the reason

i used to wake up in the morning,

the reason i would do

honestly anything at all.

i gained the reason

i love myself

and if i didn't lean inwards,

i'd have nothing left.

108

songs lost their rhythm

they're just noise now

and a dissociated sense

of mind

-without you

109

if i could feel peace again

maybe life would be beautiful

but it's chaotic in here

and i need out

110

nobody has told me

"it's going to be okay"

and meant it

because how could anyone

know if this will be okay?

-i don't blame them, i just want to feel better. i
yearn for peace in my mind. i yearn for how it used
to be. i miss being told that it'll be okay, and
knowing it actually will.

111

did you mean it?

or were you trying to spare me?

did you mean it?

or were you giving me the façade?

the fake version of you?

the one i thought was real?

112

wouldn't it have been easier

if you had just prefaced it with

the fact you hate me.

it would have saved us so much time,

so much confusion.

you should have just looked me in the eyes

and told me you hated me on our first date,

i was going to find out one way or another

and no,

i didn't expect to find out you hated me the way i
did

i wish you let me down easier

i don't know why you had to take every piece of
my peace and everything i loved at some point

i don't know how you could have stripped me of
everything in the eyes of love that was actually hate

113

honestly?

i'm tired of being positive,

putting on the show.

i'm not sure there is any positivity left in my body,

any smile left to have

it is exhausting to keep up with,

i want to let go of the act

i wish i knew how not to mask it

how not to put on the fake smile

how not to keep going

how not to fool everyone

--

was that too honest?

114

maybe i should just go to sleep

maybe i should just shut the fuck up

i've exhausted my options,

which wasn't a very extensive list

it's like everyone hears it but nobody actually does
at all

i started talking to my voice memos,

which probably could have just been left unsaid

all my words seep into the void

like a breath wasted,

words that should've never left my thoughts

i should just be quiet more often

115

my words are overflowing

i just have too much to say

and nowhere to say it

sometimes i hear nothing

but these days, my brain doesn't allow silence

it goes and goes

nonstop

i can't breathe.

i can't even move.

there is no room for anything

but noise

and nonsense

i just want to heal

116

i used to love oceans but now i think

you could probably fill oceans with

my rage

and i think i would drown

in every single one of them

i wouldn't even try to save myself

in fact,

i am already suffocating in my own anger

and i cannot pull myself out of the water

for long enough

to confront what you did to me

117

i genuinely used to consider myself

the happiest girl in the world

i'm really not anymore though,

i never thought i would turn into the girl

who forgot how to smile,

only a few years after claiming

to be the happiest girl in the world

118

fuck you honestly

i don't owe anything to anyone while i'm learning how to heal

i don't need to explain

why i don't want to talk

why i don't want to do anything with anyone

i don't need to explain why i am healing the way i am

i am just trying to survive

119

it takes a lot

to be where you are

and not let life

consume you.

it takes a lot

to get up everyday

and be the

person you are.

-i am proud of you

120

one day you will

turn around

and see the person you are

right now

from an older,

and wiser perspective

and it will make more sense

as to why it was

the way it was.

-the hard days are relative

third quarter.

121

<u>awareness</u>

to shield yourself

from pain

is to

shield yourself

from light

that may be

trying to come through

122

i could give you all the reasons

you should never fall in love again—

there is so much pain

and grief

that comes with heartbreak

but,

there is so much love

and warmth

that comes with falling.

-i still believe

123

you laid next to me and asked me where i got my hyper-independence,

my need to be alone and do it well.

i looked at you and talked about all the things growing up that rewired my brain.

and all the times i had no other option but to survive on my own,

all of these things are true,

they did force me to be extremely independent.

but i didn't tell you—

i didn't tell you how even though more times than not i am overly independent.

i was begging to feel love and fall deep and hard,

and once i did, i knew it'd be hard to get me back out.

i didn't tell you that because i thought i'd scare you away—

i thought my chances of love and leaving behind
my hyper-independence was going to shatter in
front of me.

i didn't tell you how all i've ever wanted was to feel
secure and madly in love and how i have always
been the biggest hopeless romantic.

nobody wants to hear about love and intense
vulnerability their first time lying in bed with
someone.

124

if i was asked this question all over again,

how i got my hyper-independence,

i would preface the answer by telling them

how i met a guy and told him about how i grew up
and had to be alone at times and was shoved into
independence.

i would explain the story of how i fell in love and
lost the ability to be independent,

how i cornered myself and relied

on love to get me by.

i would tell the story of how i smacked the ground
and fell so hard out of love,

and stared independence in the face again.

that would be today's answer.

125

i have not been one to know balance,

in really any aspect of my life

it's too hard to not be all or nothing

intensely, madly in love

or not at all.

i look at love as black and white

you either love someone or you don't

i don't know where the center line is,

there has to be one.

there has to be a line in between giving your all,
giving your individuality and not loving the person
at all.

-the line is probably what healthy love is supposed
to look like and i have never seen nor experienced
that before.

126

and as i wait for you,

i will continue on—

i will build the version of me

that is open for you

the version of me accepting of love

and ready to take on a new life,

a new meaning to a fulfilled life.

127

every day goes by

and i think about what my future will look like,

what the lucky one will look like,

if they'll be the person i envision

when i read poetry—

soft, well mannered, full of life, enough stories to
last a lifetime, put-together but a little rough
around the edges, wise and well-spoken.

128

i correlate poetry with music

as my fingers dance across the keyboard,

creating beautiful strings of words,

i feel like i am playing the piano

in the middle of a quiet mall on a rainy day in may,

that's how i feel when i write poetry,

like a beautiful composer with nobody listening.

129

you can have everything

and still feel

as though you have nothing

-if there is a void in your heart, you need to fill it

130

the rain patters along my window,

the window i didn't put in,

in a house i barely live in,

one that doesn't feel like home—

and all that i can think about

is how much i miss

feeling at home,

-find me a home

131

beyond the physicality,

there is so much more

the thoughts swallow me whole

they eat at the logic in my brain

and spit out the realism,

leaving me with nothing

but the romanticization of you

and what was

-faltered sense of reality

132

when you feel homeless mentally,

they said to find home in a person

but you evicted me

133

your voice was soft as yarn,

strand some together

and build a blanket of warmth,

multiple layers of comfort

and reassurance,

but i unwound under you

and everything unfolded

there's nothing left

other than a pile of unwound string

and a girl with a sad heart

134

i feel everything

and nothing

all at once

like a strange conundrum

i don't even understand

and i'm afraid

nobody will really

ever understand me

if i can't understand myself.

135

another day passes

and i feel as though

time is running out

to establish myself,

as if i'm behind

on something

time only tells

136

things are supposed to just fall into place. i'm not sure why i like to rush everything and think it is a good idea to force the universe to show me where i am supposed to be, why i think it's a good idea to force things into my life that don't actually fit and sit around, wondering why it feels painful and uncertain. that uncertain feeling you feel in your gut is a huge teller that something is out of place, something doesn't quite fit and maybe it isn't supposed to. maybe it isn't the right timing or maybe it is the right timing but the wrong thing you're going after, or the wrong person you're trying to place into your life. i am not sure what might be wrong but i do know that something is wrong with it. there's only so much in life to plan, to ask for. and the rest is to just be. that's the beauty of life, the simple existence.

137

if i could take back the

things i said,

the reassurance i gave you,

the love i expressed,

i wouldn't

because it taught me

to use it sparingly.

138

there's a soft side of me, not many people get to
meet. she's kind, she writes poetry and listens to
classical music. she falls in love with strangers and
loves nothing more than a random conversation
with someone new. she dreams of finding love and
building a beautiful life. she's soft, and loves life.
her feminine energy is reserved and patient.

-waiting for someone to bring her out

139

i think it's time for me to admit,

i miss my family

the sound of the garbage cans rolling down the
driveway on a sunday morning

the footsteps of my dad coming home from work

there was always food in the house

and i miss that.

there was always a warm hug,

a room away

i even miss the silly arguments,

and all the irritation

that comes with sharing blood

it's so weird adjusting to loneliness,

i find myself talking on the phone most waking
moments,

i miss always going home to someone,

always having an ear that will listen.

it's so weird cooking for myself,

not always having food in the pantry

and coming home to cold wooden floors

and quiet.

140

and when you hear me,

i hope you are listening—

with your head and your heart.

and when you hear me,

i hope you see me,

deeply and completely.

to be understood is to be loved

and to be listened to is to be seen

141

a cold and windy night in the city

sounds miserable to most.

walking miles, waltzing around aimlessly

he would have never done that with me,

but you did.

soft and passionate kisses in the street,

something i have always dreamed of

it's probably laughable, even,

that a girl would dream of being kissed in the middle of a busy street,

but you did, too.

 losing sight of all the people

and fully taking in your eyes

as if they were the only thing bringing air to my lungs,

the only thing my eyes could focus on,

were yours

142

i could be asked on hundreds of dates,

i could be called pretty by the most beautiful men
in the world,

i could do all the things we did,

with someone else

i could laugh with someone else

or meet up in random cities with someone else

-but it wouldn't be you

143

if i just let you in,

will you promise to be in,

and not halfway out.

144

you're like the rain, i think,

the soft pitter-patter rain,

the kind that is comforting

like a warm kiss on the cheek

bringing me in close

and holding me tight

145

you can't tell me that you don't feel it too

i know you do

there was passion,

not the kind you can fake

the kind that feels like a dream

in which i have yet to wake

146

-if it isn't real, i hope you let me believe it is for as long as possible. this isn't a feeling i ever want to not feel. and if we chose to let it go, i hope it's mutual and not crushing. i hope it's easy and simple. the thought of it not being real makes me hope that you would never let me know if it meant nothing to you. just allow me to feel what i feel, allow me to romanticize it.

147

what is it?

it's you

i just can't help but to smile around you

148

maybe it isn't real—

but there's a version of it that is real

inside my writing

so i will continue to write about us here,

it's a safe place for us to exist,

even if we don't in reality

-i need this version of us to exist, at least somewhere

149

sharing glances

exchanging quick looks

as if neither of us notice the other

and i will pack my belongings and leave

never seeing you again

150

dating has become only a nature of the apps,

a fake sense of love

too readily available

it becomes not real

-i hope i find you in physicality

full moon.

151

everything is sped up now

the beauty in slowness has faded

and romance is often made up

somewhere in between the screen

and an app

152

what i hate about love

is the lack of control,

the lack of say we have in it—

love chooses us without regard

there are no plans,

love is its own beast

and i succumb myself to it

every time

-i hope love choses the right one for me next time

153

i would count the distance between

you and i

through the little things

pinching us together each

little thing at a time

154

if i could close the gap between

you and i

i'd promise my loyalty

and swear into your heart

-cross my heart

and hope to love

155

the bad thing is i can't slow down. i long for love
and security more than anything else in the world. i
love connection i love authenticity and i love love. i
love being in love and loving someone. i love it all.
i love the falling the chase the uncertainty the fear
the reassurance the... all of it. i love love.

156

and how do i tell myself

that i am walking a fine line

of love and hurt

one step sideways

and it's over

or it's forever

-equally as scary

157

all i ask is that you hold it safely,

my heart, that is.

i ask that you treat her with

tender love

and if you decide to pass her off,

do it carefully.

-all i ask is that you aren't reckless with my heart

158

and if i am one of many

i'd rather be none of them

-don't even consider me if i'm not the only one

159

i hate to admit how inspired i am as a writer when i
have someone in my life. because most of the time,
i know they are temporary but i still write about
them because my mind fills up with thoughts and
nowhere to put them, they aren't someone i can
share the thoughts with because i know i am just
over-romanticizing everything to do with me and
you so i will shut up and paint our love story in
poems i will probably never release, hoping you
will find your way to me in your physicality.

160

it's hard to judge you for anything

i have such a clouded,

bias, version of you in my head

and i can't tell if

you are good for me

or if

you are very dangerous

161

we have the electricity

i've only ever read about,

the kind i didn't think was possible

the kind i wished for

but realistically would never have

-are you even real?

162

maybe you're just my muse

the only reason we have crossed paths

is to create something beautiful

and walk away

allow its value to only be held in space

the legend to be carried on in poetry

a story to not be spoken

yet to be read

163

i'll trade you,

i'll lend you my love

in exchange

for yours

164

if i could paint a picture of what it feels like to be
with you

i would start with the piano in the background

playing moving music

and i would add in the light in your eyes

the lust you could only feel in the air

and i'd show innocence through our laughter

i swear it's contagious

i would illustrate our spontaneity

and capture the beauty

of you and i

-what are we doing anyway? are we just here to
create art?

165

love can only be felt

not seen

but i swear i can see it in you

166

i listened when you said you just didn't want to
stress,

you wanted easy and simple

the type of love without many tests

when you said it's been hard in the past,

nobody takes you seriously

and you want something to actually last

that your career is important to you,

and you need someone to understand that

hopefully relate to you, too

and maybe i listened too much,

put you above my own needs,

lowering my standards honestly a bunch

i hoped you would care a little more—

follow through with your promises and

let me understand your heart, at its core.

167

93 miles per hour down the highway,

yes, i was checking

i wanted to see if you heard me when i spoke

or if my safety was just at play

my quietness speaks volume for the level of
comfort

i wish you would stop prying,

instead, just hear me fully

not try to distort

168

and so you're safe here

close your eyes,

dream about where you wish you were

i know it isn't here lying next to me

all i can think is that

you know it just can't be

it probably isn't us

and ill force it until my knuckles go numb

and my heart is full of dust.

169

i'm at odds with myself

i can't decipher the difference between

fear and reality

love and lust

hate and discomfort

so i lie awake

and wait for the moon to tell me

-moon sign

170

so i confess

i lied

and i wish i did less.

-safe guarding my heart

171

there isn't a single thing

i allow myself to forget

everything has importance

you just don't see that

172

a mind full of thoughts

is only as good

as the listener

173

my mind is like an empty warehouse,

sitting on a lot of value

loud and quiet all at once

a weird conundrum

between potential and waste

174

so i'll watch the world go by

without you

and i'll rack my brain

with all the times i wish

you could be here for the world

to pass by with

-i'm not supposed to be experiencing this all alone

175

i'll count the days since our last

and as the count goes up,

the chances of it being me and you

goes down exponentially.

and someday,

i'll be okay.

so how do i tell everyone after you that you will always play in the back of my mind? how do i tell them all they don't stand a chance unless they are better than you? how do i lie next to anyone else and try to forget about you? i can replace you physically but, in my brain, i will never replace you. so how will i do it? do you feel the way i feel? do men even see situations the same way that girls do? do they even care? do they even fully fall in love? do they even want love? do they even view it as sacred too? do they even want to lie awake and fall in love as they count your eyelashes? do they even count the breaths you take while in deep sleep to try and gauge if the dreams are good? do they count the heartbeats in between the sleepless breaths that you take? or is all of that the girls responsibility? is it the woman's responsibility to fall in love while the man does everything in his power to not? where is the man in all of this? is it all a façade is it all a dream or a nightmare or what the fuck is this?

177

so i take it

that it was all fake

you just wanted to see if i would break

under you and pretend it was fate

178

it was never an even playing field,

was it?

you let me say that and believe it

when all you wanted was

to be above me.

179

there's too many side factors

i can't figure out how to delete

and my only alternative

is to figure out how to compete

-why is love a competition of who is the fastest not
the most fit?

180

so i'll let you speak

and when it's my turn

i won't say a thing

-women are prettier when they're silent

part two: rem.
-i meet you in my dreams

181

is it all for nothing?

the cost of my feelings

far outweighs

what they sow

yet i still put them on the line

182

i obsess.

i never let anything go

every girl you have ever mentioned

i practically know everything about

it is exhausting.

183

in 10 years,

when i am a famous poet,

i'll look back on when you told me

to never give up on it

even if it's going nowhere

-but it's going somewhere now

184

as i sit inside this café

and my heart is plummeting through my body,

i remember that life goes on—

as everyone else here

is existing,

living a completely different life than me

so unaware of all the thoughts

circling my mind

185

january 7

i find you filling my thoughts a lot these days

and i think i'm okay with it

186

i get asked a lot if i'm lonely—

if the move, the new job, living alone,

gets to me at all

but the truth is,

for the first time in my life

the world is at my fingertips.

-alone but not lonely

187

looking at you makes me want to believe in god

and i'm not religious by any means

but someone of your nature

had to be crafted by god

-the only explanation

188

i was never one to be swooned

jaded by bullshit

and lack of authenticity

but i think you swooned me

in the least artificial way

in a magnetic pull towards you

type of way

189

i turn over and watch you sleep

the romantic in me comes out

and i hope you don't notice my promise i failed to keep

that i wouldn't be too nice, too soon

or in too deep

-maybe this time it's different

190

there are so many opportunities, and that keeps me up at night. i can only think about the countless amount of people you can meet, or the places you can decide to go. it's endless. it overwhelms me and brings me comfort all in one. as i stroll into the city and connect with strangers, and you tell me to be careful and more reserved, i made a promise to myself to not miss an opportunity to connect.

-you never know who's out there

191

hard and soft
a juxtaposition between
desire and devotion

gentle and sweet
i'll learn every little thing
about you as our souls meet

loud and confident
nobody will ever be left to question,
there's no room for distraction in how we
complement

reliant and strong
i'll hold my own when it's my time
and lean on you when it's yours

-the observer

192

how many strands in between

each freckle

i think at night

and how many ridges make up

each fingerprint

i think at night

and how many thoughts

circle your mind

as you lay at night

and how many times

do you think about me

during the day?

193

is it a nighttime thing? is it all made up? the
nighttime is for seeing you and the daytime is filled
with romanticizing the night before and filling in
any of the gaps that you missed. i spend my days
using my thoughts to fill the void that you couldn't
and sometimes i lay awake and look at the sky and
beg for the void to be filled with something other
than the moon and the stars. i ask for the sun to
come up again.

194

learn me like your favorite song

the chorus

the climax

sing me like your favorite song

in the car

in the shower

when nobody's listening

and with all your friends

195

if i could crawl inside your skin

i would

you could never pull me close enough

until i am one with you

-i dream of our unity

196

take me to a place you know. but only one that
you've never taken anyone to before. take me
somewhere you love, that you think i will too. take
me somewhere we can make ours. and if we fail, i'll
go there every day in hopes to find you all over
again.

-if it's not us in this lifetime, it's us in another one

197

wring me out

like your dirty laundry

release all my saturation

and hang me up

put me on display

in your closet

and wear me every day

198

would you choose me?

if you had all the options in the world

if you had all the money you could have

if you knew the coolest people

and everything in your life was solved

would you choose me?

-am i only here for now?

199

instead of counting sheep

i'll count the rise and fall of your chest

one

      two

            three

                  four

instead of counting sheep

ill count your worries

                  four

            three

      two

one

and hope i'm taking them away

-you take my worries away and give me breath in
my lungs

200

you are everything

i could have dreamed

and more

you are everything

a girl could want

and more

you are everything

i hope to have

for forever

and more.

-will we stand the test of time?

201

to chose

in a world of indecision

infidelity present

almost respected even,

to choose to love

at a higher risk

in a world full of accessibility

where's the line

where can I choose

and be chosen

202

nobody has ever asked

if i've ate today

before you

nobody has looked at me

with actual care

before you

nobody has liked

what i like

before you

-unmatched

203

20s are weird

i find myself so guarded

yet so open

a year ago today i was begging to leave home

now i miss home more than anything,

i find myself so lonely

yet so at peace

trying to find my niche

like i want to discover who i am

but the 'myself' part is

often intimidating—

somehow simultaneously,

i'm scared of myself

yet so sure.

204

if you could let go fully,

what part of yourself would you want to hold
onto?

what part would you want to hold back from?

to not go all out?

-where are your reservations?

205

not everything has a time

somethings stretch out,

like the world is sparing us

and telling us to wait for the sublime.

not everything is shiny and perfect

somethings are cased in imperfections

and given only when your gratefulness

radiates through the defects.

-i trust

206

my patience is wearing thin. it's been months now. i blinked and lost track of time and i've been out here on my own for months. when does it get easier? when does it lessen up? when do i feel like this is my life now, and not a temporary situation? when does it settle in? when do i make the friends i was supposed to meet? when do all the things i promised myself come to me? i'm tired of waiting. i'm impatient.

207

i'll inhale you like a cigarette
quick and fully, like i really need you
begging your air to get into my lungs
and intoxicate me with your being

i'll rewind you like a cassette
play you on a stereo in an old car
i rented just to feel close to you,
you're the only person worth seeing

i'll wait for you as i pay off worldly debt
paying off as i go,
knowing my end goal is you
and for you i'm always fiending

my time with you is not yet,

i tell myself over and over

as i pray to god for you every night

knowing he will redeem you for me

208

everyone is so picked over,

except for you

i think people have tried to pick you,

from time to time

but you pick them over

there's only room for me

right?

209

there's loss everywhere,

if you see it that way

you can lose everything

until you realize

the universe is returning you with

something greater

210

maybe i would miss you,

if my brain would allow it

maybe i should have let the kiss linger more

instead of letting you walk out the door

maybe i would miss you

if time allowed silence

and loneliness met me back with you

but my busyness takes you away

and i thank god for that

maybe i would miss you

if i stayed silent enough to have heard you speak

and not exchanged feelings for silence,

when they weren't fully at their peak

maybe i would miss you

if we ever gave it an honest try

and didn't keep everything at base level

but somehow

i find myself, now and then, still allowed to cry

211

if i lose you

i hope it's someone else's gain

you're too good

for someone not to know you

212

meet me here tomorrow

same place same time

different story

and see where it goes

even if it slips away

let it go somewhere

-remaining stale is an injustice

live passionately.